Journaling Advantage: A Guide for Men to Improve Mental Health and Manage Emotions

Oxrevolution

Published by Oxrevolution, 2023.

While every precaution has been taken in the preparation of this book, the publisher assumes no responsibility for errors or omissions, or for damages resulting from the use of the information contained herein.

JOURNALING ADVANTAGE: A GUIDE FOR MEN TO IMPROVE MENTAL HEALTH AND MANAGE EMOTIONS

First edition. May 19, 2023.

ISBN: 979-8223138433

Written by Oxrevolution.

This book is dedicated to all the males out there who are on a path of self-discovery and emotional improvement.

Introduction

Journaling is a simple and effective exercise that may have a big beneficial influence on mental health. Journaling has been substantiated in several inquiries to support with pressure operation, spirit modulation, and altogether well- being. Nevertheless, despite these benefits, some men may be hesitant to begin journaling due to certain barriers.

As a man, I was hesitant to start a journaling practice due to various barriers. Still, after I started writing, I realized it was a simple yet effective hobby horse that had a major impact on my internal health. Journaling has assisted me with stress management, mood regulation, and overall well-being.

I was free to express myself without fear of condemnation via journaling. It helped me to think on my experiences and get a better knowledge of myself. Writing down my thoughts also helped me to identify patterns and triggers that affected my mood and behavior.

I found that journaling was a great tool for managing my stress levels. I found that journaling was a great tool for managing my stress levels. Whenever I felt overwhelmed or nervous, I would write down my thoughts and passions, which helped me reuse my feelings and lessen my stress situations.

Overall, journaling has been a precious tool for perfecting my internal health and well- being. It has helped me gain a better understanding of myself, manage my stress situations, and regulate my feelings. I would largely recommend journaling to anyone, anyhow of their gender, who's looking for a simple yet effective way to ameliorate their internal health.

The benefits of journaling for mental health

ONE OF THE MOST SIGNIFICANT benefits of journaling is that it can help individuals gain sapience into their studies and feelings. By writing down their studies, individualities can gain a better understanding of their feelings, identify patterns in their thinking, and gain clarity on their values and precedences. This can help individualities manage stress, ameliorate their mood, and enhance their overall mental health.

Common barriers to journaling for men

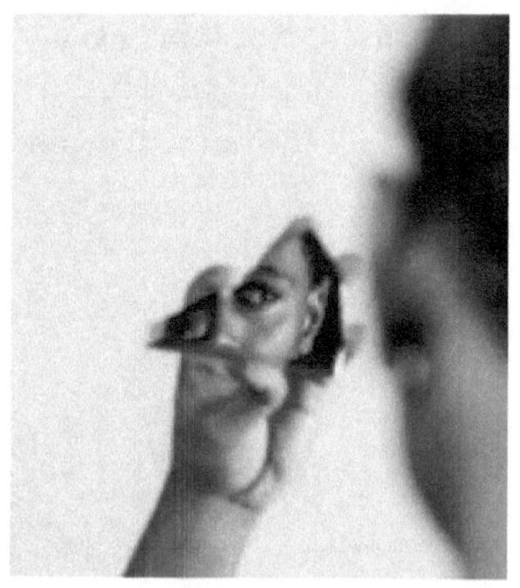

STILL, DESPITE THESE benefits, numerous men may feel reluctant to start a journaling practice. One common hedge is societal prospects around masculinity. Men may feel pressure to suppress their feelings and prioritize action over soul-searching. Also, some men may feel that journaling isn't a socially respectable exertion for them or that it may be seen as a sign of weakness or vulnerability.

Another hedge to journaling may be a lack of knowledge or understanding about how to get started. Men may not be familiar with the different approaches to journaling or may feel doubtful about what to write. They may also struggle to find the time and provocation to start a regular journaling practice.

Despite these walls, journaling can be a precious tool for men who want to ameliorate their mental health and manage their feelings. By breaking down these walls and furnishing practical tips and tools, men can learn to incorporate journaling into their diurnal routine and enjoy the numerous benefits that it can offer.

Chapter 1 Understanding the Science Behind Journaling

Journaling is more than simply a pastime; it is also backed by science. In this chapter, we will explore the science behind journaling and understand how it can appreciatively impact mental health.

How journaling affects the brain:

WHEN AN INDIVIDUAL journals, they engage in a process of self-reflection, which activates specific areas of the brain. Research has shown that journaling can help stimulate neural exertion in the prefrontal cortex, which is responsible for decision-making, problem solving, and emotional regulation. By engaging in this process, individualities can enhance their cognitive functioning and promote better internal health.

.

Here are five practical examples of how journaling can impact the brain:

1. Boosting creativity: Writing allows individuals to tap into their inner thoughts and ideas, helping them become more creative and innovative.

2. Reducing stress: By writing down their thoughts, individuals can release pent-up emotions and reduce stress levels.

3. Enhancing memory: Journaling can help improve memory and cognitive function by stimulating neural activity in the brain.

4. Perfecting sleep: By releasing thoughts onto paper, individuals can clear their minds and promote better sleep quality.

5. Boosting overall well- Being regular journaling can help individuals develop a more positive mindset and ameliorate their overall sense of well- being.

The link between journaling and emotional regulation:

JOURNALING CAN ALSO play an essential part in emotional regulation. By writing down their thoughts and feelings, individuals can identify patterns and triggers that lead to negative feelings. This can help individualities regulate their feelings and manage their responses to stressful situations.

Here are five practical illustrations of how journaling can help with emotional regulation

1. Associating triggers: By writing down their feelings, individualities can identify patterns and triggers that lead to negative feelings.

2. Developing managing strategies: Journaling can help individualities develop effective managing strategies to manage stress and negative feelings.

3. perfecting self- awareness: By reflecting on their thoughts and feelings, individuals can develop a lesser sense of self- awareness, which can lead to better emotional regulation.

4. Enhancing communication: Journaling can help individuals express their feelings more effectively, perfecting communication with others.

5. Promoting adaptability: Regular journaling can help individuals develop adaptability, enabling them to bounce back from challenging situations.

In summary, understanding the science behind journaling is essential for understanding how it can appreciatively impact internal health. By boosting brain conditioning and promoting emotional regulation, journaling can be a precious tool for individuals looking to ameliorate their overall well- being.

Chapter 2 Overcoming Barriers to Journaling

While journaling can have a profound impact on internal health, numerous individuals may feel reluctant to start a journaling practice due to various hedges. In this chapter, we will explore common hedges to journaling and practical tips for prostrating them.

Addressing societal expectations around masculinity:

ONE COMMON HEDGE TO journaling for men is societal prospects around masculinity. Masculinity can be defined as a set of traits or characteristics generally associated with men, similar as strength, durability, and independence. While some of these traits can be positive, there's a risk in believing that men must cleave to a narrow description of masculinity in order to be considered" real men." It's conceivable for men to suffer substantial pressure and strain when they perceive a sense of duty to constantly parade their masculinity to the world.

This can produce a grueling situation for men who feel the need to conform to societal prospects regarding what it means to be mannish. Cultivating a healthy sense of masculinity involves embracing positive traits while also being open to vulnerability and emotional expression. This can help men more navigate life's challenges and enhance their overall well being.

Some ways that men can cultivate positive masculinity include:

1. Building healthy relationships: forming close bonds with other men and women can help men develop empathy and emotional intelligence, which are important traits for particular growth and well- being.

2. Pursuing physical health engaging in regular physical exertion can help men stay healthy and maintain a positive body image, which can ameliorate tone- regard and overall internal health.

3. Practicing emotional regulation:learning to honor and manage feelings can help men navigate delicate situations and make healthy connections by embracing the power of journaling and rehearsing awareness.

4. Developing a sense of purpose:setting pretensions and working towards them can give men a sense of purpose and fulfillment, which can ameliorate overall well- being.

It's important to note that masculinity doesn't have to be rigorously defined, nor does it have to be a fully separate reality from femininity. Both men and women can profit from embracing positive traits associated with both masculinity and femininity, similar as empathy, emotional intelligence, and fierceness. By combining both masculinity and femininity traits, individuals can completely express themselves and lead fulfillinglives.Men may feel pressure to suppress their feelings and prioritize action over soul-searching. This can make journaling feel like an uncomfortable or indeed an impossible exercise.

Here are five practical examples of how to address societal prospects around masculinity:

1. Challenge traditional ideas of masculinity: Recognize that masculinity isn't limited to traditional gender capacities and that journaling is an important tool for emotional regulation.

2. Encourage vulnerability: Embrace vulnerability and recognize that it's a sign of strength rather than weakness.

3. Find a probative community: Connect with other men who value emotional intelligence and encourage each other to journal.

4. Recognize the benefits: Educate yourself on the multitudinous benefits of journaling, similarly as improving mental health and enhancing self mindfulness.

5. Be patient: Remember that breaking down traditional ideas of masculinity takes time, and that it's okay to feel uncomfortable or vulnerable when starting a journaling practice.

Finding the time and motivation to journal:

ANOTHER BARRIER TO journaling is finding the time and motivation to start a regular practice. Many individuals may feel overwhelmed by their busy schedules or struggle with self-discipline.

Here are five practical examples of how to find the time and motivation to journal:

1. Produce a routine: Schedule time for journaling each day or week, and make it a harmonious part of your routine.

2. Start small: Begin with short journaling sessions and gradually increase the quantum of time as you come more comfortable.

3. Set purposes : Establish specific purposes for your journaling practice, similar as writing about a particular content or exploring a specific emotion.

4. Find inspiration: Seek out inspiration and provocation from other journalers or from resources similar to books or blogs.

5. Use prompts: Use prompts or guided journaling exercises to help you get started and stay motivated.

Overcoming self- mistrust and negative self- talk:

EVENTUALLY, NUMEROUS individuals may struggle with self- mistrust or negative self- talk when starting a journaling practice. They may feel doubtful about their writing capacities or fear judgment from others.

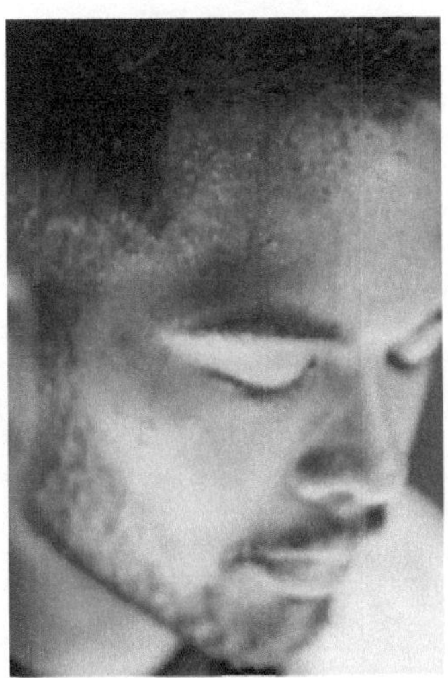

Here are five practical examples of how to overcome self- distrust and negative self- talk:

1. Embrace fault: Recognize that journaling is a particular practice and that there's no" right" or" wrong" way to do it.

2. Exercise self- compassion: Be kind to yourself and recognize that miscalculations or lapses are a natural part of the process.

3. Challenge negative thoughts: Recognize when negative tone- talk is creeping in and challenge it with positive declarations.

4. Use visualization techniques: Fantasize yourself successfully journaling and achieving your aspirations.

5. Celebrate progress: Celebrate small successes along the way and fete the progress you have made.

In summary, while there may be walls to journaling, with practical tips and a willingness to try new approaches, individuals can overcome these obstacles and enjoy the numerous benefits of a regular journaling practice.

Chapter 3 Different Approaches to Journaling

There are several ways to journaling, and determining which one works best for you might be vital in developing a regularhabit.In this chapter, we'll look into three regular journaling approaches and extend some practicable tips for getting started.

Gratitude Journaling:

GRATITUDE JOURNALING involves writing down things that Gratitude journaling involves writing down effects that you're thankful for in your life.

This can be an important tool for perfecting moods and overall well being. By implementing this approach it can also increase self-awareness and emotional management.

Here are five practical examples of how to incorporate gratitude journaling into your practice:

1. Write down three effects you're thankful for each day, no matter how small.

2. Reflect on a grueling situation and identify something positive that came out of it.

3. Focus on people in your life who have made a positive impact and write down why you're thankful for them.

4. Take a walk in nature and write down what you're thankful for in the atmosphere around you.

5. Before bed, reflect on your day and write down one thing that went well and why you're thankful for it.

Reflective Journaling:

REFLECTIVE JOURNALING involves exploring your thoughts and feelings in a non-judgmental way. This approach can help increase self-mindfulness and promote emotional regulation.

Here are five practical examples of how to incorporate reflective journaling into your practice:

1. Reflect on a recent event and note down your thoughts and passions about it.

2. Write about a current challenge you are facing and explore different perspectives on how to approach it.

3. Write a letter to yourself, expressing compassion and understanding towards yourself.

4. Reflect on a personal value or belief and explore how it influences your daily life.

5. Make a note of the things that are causing you stress and look into strategies to remedy them.

Free Writing:

FREE WRITING INVOLVES writing continuously for a set period of time, without fussing about the alphabet or structure. This approach can help promote creativity and reduce self- suppression.

Here are five practical examples of how to incorporate free writing into your practice:

1. Set a timekeeper for 10 minutes and write continuously about whatever comes to mind.

2. Write a sluice- of- awareness piece about a particular content or issue.

3. Use a writing prompt to start your free writing, similar as" I remember when."

4. Even if you do not intend to partake it, write a letter to someone important or who has had a big effect on your life.

5. Experiment with different writing mediums, similar to pen and paper or digital writing tools.

Prompts and Exercises to Get Started:

Using prompts is a simple and effective way to kickstart your journaling trip.

A prompt is a specific content or question that serves as a starting point for your writing. It gives you a focus and direction, ruling out the blank runner pattern and helping you overcome any scribe's block you may have.

Prompts can be broad or specific, allowing you to explore various aspects of your life or concentrate on a particular theme. These can give structure and guidance for your writing practice.

Here are five practical examples of prompts and exercises to get started:

1. Write about an important incident in your life and how it influenced you pouring all your heart.

2. Make a list of stuff you're proud of and explore why they're important to you.

3. Write a letter to your future self, expressing your possibilities and dreams.

4. Reflect on a quote or lyric that resonates with you and explore why.

5. Write a" sluice of awareness" piece about a particular emotion, similar to fear or sadness.

In summary, there are numerous different approaches to journaling, and finding the one that works everyday for you is a matter of trial and error. By exploring different approaches and incorporating prompts and exercises, individuals can develop a satisfying and fulfilling journaling practice.

Chapter 4 Using Journaling to Manage Specific Mental Health Challenges

Journaling can be a useful tool for handling specific mental health challenges similar to anxiety, depression, and trauma. In this chapter, we will explore each of these challenges and how journaling can be used to treat symptoms.

Anxiety:

ANXIETY IS A MENTAL health condition characterized by inordinate worrying, fear, and unease. Symptoms can include contending thoughts, restlessness, and difficulty concentrating. Journaling can be a helpful tool for managing anxiety by providing a way to express and process delicate emotions.

Here are five practical examples of how to use journaling to manage anxiety:

1. Write down your worries and fears in detail, and also contest them by writing out substantiation to the negative.

2. Make a list of your triggers for anxiety and develop managing strategies for each one.

3. Write a letter to your anxiety, expressing your dissatisfaction and vowing to take control.

4. Reflect on occasions when you have successfully managed your anxiety and write down the strategies that worked.

5. Use mindfulness methods to concentrate on the present moment and write down your observations and sensations.

Depression:

DEPRESSION IS A MENTAL health condition characterized by patient feelings of sadness and forlornness. Symptoms can include loss of interest in activities, fluctuations in appetite, and experiencing insomnia. Journaling can be a conducive tool for managing depression by furnishing a way to express emotions and pinpoint patterns in the thinking garden.

Here are five practical ways to utilize journaling to cope with depression:

1. Write down your thoughts and feelings when you're feeling low, and also dispute negative thoughts with substantiation to the negative.

2. Make a list of activities that bring you gladness and make a plan to integrate them into your routine.

3. Write a letter to your future self, imagining a time when you have successfully overcome your depression.

4. Reflect on occasions when you have felt fortunate and write down the factors that pitched into those feelings.

5. Use mindfulness methods to concentrate on the present moment and write down your observations and senses. .

Trauma:

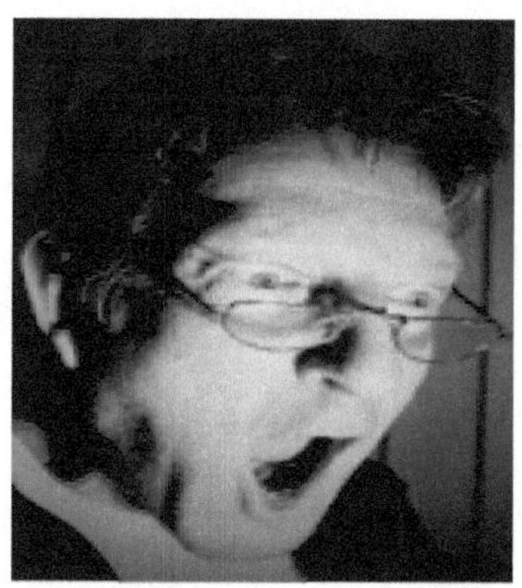

TRAUMA IS A PSYCHOLOGICAL and emotional response to a stressful or disturbing incident or experience that surpasses a person's capability to control or deal with.Intrusive thoughts, flashbacks, and hypervigilance are illustrations of symptoms. Journaling may be an effective system for managing trauma because it provides a secure area to explore feelings and process grueling memories

Here are five practical ways to utilize journaling to cope with trauma.

1. Write down your memories of the traumatic event, focusing on the emotions and sensations that arise.

2. Make a list of coping strategies for managing triggers, such as deep breathing or visualization exercises.

3. Write a letter to the person or people involved in the traumatic event, expressing your emotions and setting boundaries.

4. Reflect on moments when you have felt safe and write down the factors that contributed to those feelings.

5. Use mindfulness techniques to focus on the present moment and write down your observations and sensations.

In summary, journaling can be a useful tool for managing specific mental health challenges such as anxiety, depression, and trauma. By providing a safe space to express emotions and process difficult experiences, individuals can develop a greater sense of self-awareness and emotional regulation.

Chapter 5 Journaling for Relationships

Enhancing Communication:

Keeping a journal is a useful instrument for men to enhance their communication skills. Writing down their thoughts and feelings before ventilating them to others can be advantageous in gaining clarity and reducing misunderstandings. Journaling prompts can support men in reflecting on their communication patterns and identifying areas for enhancement, leading to further effective communication. This practice can enhance relationships and grease better understanding with others.

Imagine the impact journaling can have on your capability to communicate effectively. By solely taking a limited moment each day to jot down your thoughts and feelings, you can witness a profound move in how you vent yourself to those around you. Consider the times when you've felt misunderstood or plodded to articulate your feelings — journaling can give a significant solution.

To make your journaling practice more captivating and fruitful, try incorporating prompts that prompt self-reflection. For illustration, you could ask yourself questions like:

1. How did I communicate today? Were there any occasions where I felt particularly effective or ineffective in ventilating myself?
2. What feelings did I witness during my interactions with others? How did these feelings influence my communication mode?
3. Did I notice any recreating patterns in my communication? Are there any habits or tendencies I would like to modify or

upgrade?

4. How did my communication impact my relationships? Were there any cases where better communication could have led to a deeper understanding or resolution?

5. What strategies can I apply to improve my communication skills? Are there any specific areas where I would like to concentrate my efforts?

By engaging in this self-reflective rehearsal, you will gradually unfold a strengthened awareness of your communication habits and patterns. Over time, you will begin to identify areas for enhancement and apply strategies that align with your communication goals. The journal becomes a secure space for exploration, permitting you to express your thoughts without judgment and discover clarity before engaging in conversations with others.

.

Enhancing Empathy:

EMPATHY IS PIVOTAL in constructing strong relationships, and journaling can help men cultivate this skill. By reflecting on their own experiences, men can better understand the viewpoints of others, leading to prime empathy and compassion. Journaling prompts can assist men exercise empathy by encouraging them to consider other people's experiences and feelings.

Here's a simple practice for increasing empathy through journaling:

1. Choose a person or group of people who are different from you in some way(e.g., different race, gender, age, culture, faith, socioeconomic posture).

2. Spend some time researching and mastering about their experiences and perspectives. This could involve reading papers or books, watching documentaries, or talking to people who belong to the group you elected.

3. Set apart some time to reflect on what you learned. Use journaling prompts to help guide your thoughts, such as:

- What aspects of this person/group's experiences did you find most amazing?

- What emotions did you feel as you learned about their adventures?

- What insights did you pick up about their perspective?

- How might their experiences vary from your own?

- What conduct could you take to support this person/group in a significant way?

4. After journaling about your observations, think about taking action grounded on what you learnt.This might encompass volunteering, contributing to an association that supports the group you elected, or speaking with someone from that community to acquire a better understanding.

By sharing in this exertion, you may strictly exercise empathy and extend your mindfulness of others.This can help you to become a further compassionate and caring person over time, leading to lesser connections and a deeper connection to the world around you.

Resolving Conflicts:

JOURNALING CAN ALSO prop in resolving conflicts by furnishing a safe space to explore and process emotions.Men can use journaling to pinpoint the root cause of a conflict, express their emotions, and brainstorm achievable solutions.Journaling prompts can help men navigate difficult conversations and find constructive ways to settle conflicts.

Here's a useful conflict resolution exercise:

1. Identify a conflict that you're presently passing or have endured in the past. It could be a disagreement with a friend, family member, or colleague, or a more complex issue similar to a political or social conflict.

2. Set apart some time to reflect on the conflict.Use journaling prompts to help guide your thoughts, suchlike as:

- What are the underpinning issues and interests of each person involved in the conflict?

- What are your own interests and requirements in this situation?

- What feelings are you experiencing as a result of the conflict?

- How might the other person(s) be feeling?

- What assumptions or impulses might you be bringing to the conflict?

- Are there any implicit misunderstandings or miscommunications that need to be handled?

3. After you've journaled about your reflections, view ways to address the conflict.Use the following route to guide your process

- Seek to understand the other person's perspective. Approach the person with an open mind and genuinely try to hear and understand their point of view.

- Express your own requirements and interests easily and calmly. Use" I" statements to avoid blame and concentrate on your own feelings and needs.

- Brainstorm possible solutions together. Explore different options and look for ways to meet both of your requirements.

- Choose a solution and agree on the next route. Once you've linked a solution that works for both of you, make a plan to apply it and follow through on your commitments. .

4. After you've addressed the conflict, reflect on what you picked up from the experience. Use journaling prompts to help guide your thoughts, suchlike as:

- What did you pick up about yourself and the other person(s) affected in the conflict?

- What strategies were most efficient in resolving the conflict?

- What could you have done else?

- What effect has the dispute had on your connection with the other person(s)?

- What route can you take to help similar conflicts from arising in the future?

By engaging in this exercise, you can practice effective conflict resolution skills and unfold a profound accord of yourself and those who are around you. Over time, this can help you construct powerful relationships, enhance your communication skills, and produce a more peaceful and harmonious atmosphere.

Strengthening Romantic Relationships:

JOURNALING CAN BE ESPECIALLY useful in romantic relationships,where communication and empathy are essential. By journaling together, couples can deepen their emotional relation and build intimacy. Journaling prompts can help couples explore their individual and shared values, goals, and desires, strengthening their bond.

Here's a simple practice to help you build your love relationships:

1.Set apart devoted quality time with your partner. Choose a specific day or evening when you can both concentrate on each other without distractions.

2. Create a comfy and inviting atmosphere. Prepare a cozy space, whether it's at home or nearly special, where you can relax and have unbroken conversations.

3. Begin the session with open and truthful communication. Start by expressing gratitude for your significant other and the relationship you partake. Share what you appreciate about them and the ways they contribute positively to your life.

4. Take turns laboriously harkening to each other. Practice compassionate listening by giving your full attention to your significant other without interjecting or offering immediate solutions. Encourage them to partake their thoughts, passions, and concerns.

5.Engage in reflective exercises to deepen emotional connection. Use journaling prompts or questions to guide a meaningful conversation. Some examples include

- What are your visions and goals as individuals and as a couple?

- How can we better endorse each other in achieving our individual goals?

- What are our strengths as a couple, and how can we exercise them to defeat obstacles?

- How can we enrich our communication and understanding of each other's requirements?

6. Engage in an exercise that promotes shared experiences and bonding. This could be cooking a meal together, going for a walk, playing a board game, or engaging in a hobbyhorse or activity you both enjoy. The goal is to create positive memories and fortify the emotional connection.

7. Exercise affection and intimacy. Physical touch is important for keeping up a strong romantic bond. Show affection through hugs, snuggling, holding hands, or engaging in other forms of non-sexual physical intimacy.

8. Wrap up the session by venting admiration and love. Share what you value most about your significant other and the relationship. Reaffirm your commitment and express your intentions for continual growth and support in the relationship.

9. Make a commitment to apply the insights gained from the session into your day-to-day lives. Discuss specific actions or changes you both can make to enrich the relationship and support each other's requirements.

10. Regularly schedule similar sessions to remain nourishing your romantic connection. Consistency is pivotal in maintaining a strong and healthy relationship. Set a recurring date night or quality time to ensure proceeding communication, connection, and growth.

By engaging in this workable activity, you and your significant other can laboriously strengthen your romantic relationship, deepen your emotional connection, and produce a foundation of love, trust, and understanding.

Nurturing Friendships and Family Dynamics:

JOURNALING CAN ALSO be used to nurture friendships and family relationships. By sharing journal entries with loved ones, men can promote open and honest communication, deepen their understanding of each other, and strengthen their relationships. Journaling prompts can assist men explore their relationships with friends and family, identify areas for growth, and celebrate their connections.

Here's a simple practice for strengthening bonds and enhancing family dynamics:

Nurturing Friendships:

1. Identify a friend or group of buddies with whom you'd like to consolidate your connection.

2. Set aside devoted time to engage in an exercise together, similar as going for a walk, grabbing coffee, or doing a shared hobby.

3. During your time together, practice active listening. Allow your friend(s) to speak without interruptions and authentically concentrate on what they're saying.

4. Reflect on your interactions afterward. Journal about the experience applying prompts such like as:

- What did you pick up about your friend(s) during your time together?

- How did you feel while actively harkening to them?

- What common denominators or differences did you discover between you and your friend(s)?

- How can you support and encourage your friend(s) in their trials?

- What steps can you take to consolidate the fellowship and make it more significant?

5. Act on your reflections by integrating what you've learned into your future interactions. Consider reaching out to your friend(s) to extend support, plan future exercise, or solely check in on how they are going

Improving Family Dynamics:

1. Choose a family member with whom you'd like to enhance your relationship or better understand their perspective

2. Set apart a devoted time to have a one- on- one discussion with them. Choose a comfortable and private environment where you can both openly express yourselves.

3. Exercise active listening during the conversation. Show real interest and empathy by allowing the family member to speak without hiccups or judgment.

4. Reflect on the discussion afterward. Journal about it using prompts such like as

● What did you learn about your family member's experiences, feelings, or concerns?

● How did the conversation make you feel? Did it alter your viewpoint in any way?

● What commonalities or differences did you discover between you and your family member?

● How can you endorse and strengthen your relationship with this family member?

● What route can you take to address any conflicts or misunderstandings that may have got up?

5. Take action grounded on your reflections. This could involve initiating further conversations, expressing your support or understanding, or making an effort to spend additional quality time together.

Remember, constructing and nurturing relationships takes time and effort. Consistently exercising empathy, active listening, and understanding can significantly contribute to stronger friendships and healthier family dynamics.

Chapter 6 journaling for Personal Growth and Goal Setting

Journaling may be a powerful stimulus for personal development and goal attainment.This chapter looks at how journaling may improve self-awareness, assist defining personal values, set meaningful objectives, and measure progress on the personal development path.

Self-Reflection:

SELF-REFLECTION IS a critical instrument for private growth, and journaling is an effective way to grease this process. Men can employ journaling as a means of exploring their inner world, examining their thoughts, feelings, and experiences, and gaining deeper perceptivity into themselves. By reflecting regularly, individuals can develop a prime understanding of their strengths, weaknesses, values, and aspirations, which can assist them make more informed decisions and steer life's challenges with prime confidence. Journaling prompts can be used to direct men in reflecting on their particular growth journey, exploring their desired direction in life, and identifying effective routes they can take to achieve their goals. Through intentional self-reflection, men can cultivate major self-awareness and cultivate a more significant and fulfilling life.

Identifying Personal Values:

JOURNALING CAN ASSIST men clarify their core values, which serve as coaching principles for their actions and decisions. By exploring individual values through journaling, men can align their lives with what truly matters to them, leading to a prime sense of fulfillment and purpose. Journaling prompts can help men in identifying and prioritizing their values, allowing them to make choices in line with their authentic characters.

Here is a useful exercise for determining personal values:

1. Take some time to reflect on what's meaningful to you in life. What are the things that offer your life meaning and purpose? These might contain things like family, career, spirituality, individual growth, wellness, or community involvement

2.Make a list of your values. Start by brainstorming a list of words that reverberate with you, such as honesty, kindness, ingenuity, or courage. Then, narrow down your list to the top 5-10 values that are most significant to you.

3. Set your values as your top priority. Sort your values by importance, beginning with the most essential to you. This is a challenging process, but try to be honest with yourself about what is genuinely important to you.

4. Interrogate your values. Consider why each value is significant to you.How does it suit with your beliefs and goals? What consequence does it have on your thoughts and behavior?

5. Determine how you will live your ideals. Consider different methods to incorporate your principles into your daily life. For example, if kindness is one of your values, you may resolve to doing one considerate act for someone else every day.If one of your values is personal development, you could make a goal to acquire a new skill or take on a new challenge to stimulate your mind.

6. Review your values regularly. It is significant to periodically review your values and make sure they still reverberate with you.As you grow and change, your values may reposition as well. Make adaptations as

needed to ensure that your values are always aligned with who you're and what you want out of life.

Discovering and integrating your own set of individual values serves as a compass that guides your life's goal and direction. It empowers you to frame choices that reverberate with your aspirations and principles, leading to a deep sense of achievement and pleasure in all aspects of your journey.

Setting Meaningful Goals:

JOURNALING SERVES AS a precious tool for setting goals that are aligned with individual values and aspirations. Through journaling, men can define specific, measurable, attainable, applicable, and time- bound(SMART) goals. Journaling prompts can assist men break down their goals into actionable steps, establish deadlines, and produce a roadmap for success.

Here's a practical exercise for setting meaningful goals:

1.Start by considering your values and priorities. What is the most paramount thing in your life? What long-term goals do you have?

2. Brainstorm a list of implicit goals that align with your values and priorities. Do not bother about whether they seem attainable or not at this stage.

3. Refine your list of goals by considering whether they meet the succeeding criteria:

- They are specific and well-defined.

- They are measured so that you can track your development.

- They are feasible within a sensible timeframe.

- They are inline with your beliefs and priorities.

- They are demanding enough to be inspiring, but not so difficult that they are unreachable.

4. Prioritize your goals grounded on which are most significant to you and which you want to tackle first.

5. Break down your goals into less manageable steps. This will assist you make progression towards your goals without feeling overwhelmed.

6. Create a timeline for each goal, with specific milestones and deadlines. This will assist you stay on trace and hold yourself responsible.

7. Write down your goals and keep them somewhere observable, such as on a bulletin board or in a planner. This will serve as a memorial of what you are working towards and assist you stay motivated.

Consider finding an accountability mate or group to give reinforcement and encouragement as you work toward your goals to make this exertion more successful. This might be a friend, family member, or instructor who shares your views and goals. Sharing your objects with others and accepting sentiments and encouragement might increase your chances of accomplishment and make the journey to your goals more comforting.

Cultivating Motivation:

MAINTAINING MOTIVATION throughout the individual growth journey is vital. Journaling provides an outlet to explore motivations, passions, and the reasons behind pursuing certain goals. By regularly journaling about their progress, successes, and lapses, men can reinforce their motivation, celebrate milestones, and learn from challenges. Journaling prompts can assist men tap into their natural provocation, fantasize their desired outcomes, and stay concentrated on their journey.

Here's a helpful activity for increasing motivation:

1. Identify a goal or aspiration that you want to achieve. It could be related to your individual life, career, health, or any zone that's significant to you.

2. Start by reflecting on why this goal is significant to you. Journal about the reasons behind your drive to achieve it. Ask yourself

- What do you hope to gain or witness by achieving this goal?

- How will it appreciatively impact your life or the lives of others?

- What values or principles does this dream align with?

3. Break down your goal into lower, workable steps. Write them down in your journal, creating a clear roadmap of what needs to be done to attain your goal.

4. Explore potential obstacles or challenges that you may encounter along the way. Journal about them and brainstorm master plans for overcoming these hurdles. Consider the following:

- What are the possible roadblocks that may hamper your progress?

- How can you proactively maneuver these challenges?

- Who can support you or give advice when you face difficulties?

5. Reflect on your strengths and skills that can assist you succeed. Write about the capabilities and resources you hold that will contribute to achieving your goal by considering the following:

- What skills, knowledge, or experiences do you have that will be valuable?

- How can you capitalize these strengths to drive yourself forward?

- Are there any zones where you may need to cultivate new skills or seek more support?

6. Create a visual representation of your goal. This could be a vision board, a sketch, or a collage that captures the essence of what you are striving for. Place it nearly visible as a memorial of your motivation and commitment.

7. Set periodic check-in points in your journal to trace your progress. Write about your achievements, setbacks, and lessons learned along the way. Celebrate small victories and use any setbacks as openings for growth and adaptation.

8. Continuously review your journal entries to stay connected to your motivation. Revisit your original reflections on why the goal is significant to you. Use them as a source of alleviation during moments of doubt or fatigue.

Remember, motivation isn't stable, but by taking on in this exercise and regularly reflecting on your journey, you can cultivate a resilient and sustainable motivation that propels you towards your goals.

Tracking Progress:

JOURNALING ALLOWS MEN to track their progress, observe patterns, and reflect on lessons mastered along the way. By reviewing former entries, men can gain perceptivity into their growth, identify areas of enhancement, and celebrate achievements. Journaling prompts can grease self-assessment, reflection on setbacks, and planning for future actions, ensuring continual growth and development.

Here's a useful activity for keeping track of your progress in becoming more empathetic:

1. Pinpoint one or two specific conduct you want to take,to become more empathetic. This could include harkening more actively to others, trying to understand other people's viewpoints, or practicing kindness towards others.

2. Set a specific goal for each action. For illustration, if your goal is to listen more laboriously, your specific goal might be to listen without interposing for 10 minutes during a conversation.

3. Create a tracking system to cover your progress towards these goals. This could involve using a journal, a habit-tracking app, or a simple spreadsheet. Be certain to include the goal, the date, and a space to note your progress towards the goal.

4. Set a regular time to reevaluate your progress. This might be executed on a daily, weekly, or monthly basis, depending on your preferences. .

5. Reflect on your progress towards each goal. Use the succeeding questions to guide your reflections:

- What measures have you made to come closer to your goal?

- What difficulties did you confront in accomplishing your goal?

- What tactics have been most beneficial in assisting you to attain your goal?

● How have your actions influenced your connections with others?

● As a result of your acts, have you received any new ideas or perspectives?

6. Adjust your objectives or strategies as necessary. If you're having trouble making progress toward your goals, consider changing your technique or selecting a more attainable target. If you're making good progress, think about creating a new, more difficult objective to keep pushing yourself toward deeper empathy.

You may keep yourself accountable and celebrate your victories along the road by charting your progress toward being more compassionate. This can help you build greater empathy abilities and foster deeper, more meaningful interactions with people around you over time.

Chapter 7 Integrating Mindfulness and Meditation into Journaling

Within the realm of personal development, the integration of mindfulness and meditation practices with journaling can yield profound benefits. This chapter delves into the transformative combination of mindfulness, meditation, and journaling, exploring how these practices can deepen self-awareness, reduce stress, and enrich the journaling experience.

Embracing Mindfulness in Journaling:

MINDFULNESS INVOLVES being fully present in the current moment, observing thoughts, emotions, and sensations without judgment. When applied to journaling, mindfulness enhances the quality of self-reflection, allowing for a deeper exploration of inner experiences. By adopting a mindful approach to journaling, men can cultivate heightened awareness, enhance their ability to observe their thoughts and emotions objectively, and gain insights into patterns and triggers.

Here's a practical exercise that combines mindfulness with journaling:

1. Find a quiet and comfortable space where you can focus without distractions.
2. Begin by taking a few deep breaths to center yourself and bring your attention to the present moment.
3. Open your journal and write down the date and any thoughts or emotions that are currently on your mind. Allow yourself to freely express whatever comes up without judgment or editing.

4. Now, shift your focus to your physical sensations. Close your eyes and bring your awareness to your body. Notice any areas of tension, discomfort, or relaxation. Take a few moments to breathe into those areas and release any tension or tightness.

5. With your eyes still closed, bring your attention to your breath. Observe the sensation of the breath entering and leaving your body. Notice the rise and fall of your chest or the sensation of air passing through your nostrils. Allow your breath to anchor you in the present moment.

6. Begin to journal about your experience of mindfulness and how it feels to be fully present in the here and now. Reflect on the sensations in your body, the thoughts passing through your mind, and any emotions that arise during this practice.

7. As you write, explore any insights or realizations that arise from being mindful. Consider how being present in the moment impacts your perception of the world, your relationships, and your overall well-being.

8. If you encounter any resistance or distractions during the practice, acknowledge them without judgment and gently guide your attention back to the present moment.

9. Once you have finished journaling, take a moment to review what you have written. Notice any patterns, themes, or revelations that emerge from your reflections.

10. Close your journal and take a few more deep breaths, allowing yourself to integrate the experience of mindfulness and journaling.

This exercise combines the power of mindfulness with journaling to cultivate self-awareness, presence, and a deeper connection with your inner self. By regularly engaging in this practice, you can enhance your ability to be fully present in each moment and bring a mindful awareness to your journaling practice. This, in turn, can deepen your self-reflection, promote clarity of thought, and bring greater calm and focus to your daily life.

Integrating Meditation into Journaling:

MEDITATION IS A POWERFUL practice for calming the mind, cultivating focus, and fostering self-awareness. By incorporating meditation techniques into journaling, men can create a harmonious space for reflection and introspection. Techniques such as breathwork, body scan meditation, or loving-kindness meditation can be employed to anchor oneself in the present moment and establish a sense of tranquility and centeredness before engaging in journaling.

Practical Examples:

- Begin each journaling session with a brief mindfulness meditation, focusing on the breath and grounding yourself in the present moment.

- Practice a body scan meditation before journaling, systematically scanning your body from head to toe, noticing any sensations or areas of tension.

- Use a loving-kindness meditation to cultivate compassion and kindness towards yourself and others before engaging in reflective journaling.

- Practice mindful eating before journaling, savoring each bite of food and noticing the sensory experience. Then, journal about the sensations and emotions that arise during the process.

• Incorporate mindful movement, such as yoga or walking meditation, into your journaling routine, allowing the body to become a vehicle for mindfulness and inspiration.

Deepening Self-Reflection:

MINDFULNESS AND MEDITATION can deepen the process of self-reflection in journaling. By practicing mindfulness during journaling sessions, men can bring a heightened level of awareness to their thoughts, emotions, and physical sensations. This enables them to delve deeper into their experiences, uncover underlying beliefs and patterns, and gain valuable insights into their thought processes and behaviors.

Here's a practical exercise for deepening self-reflection:

1. Find a quiet and comfortable space where you can focus without distractions.

2. Begin by setting an intention for your self-reflection session. What do you hope to gain or discover about yourself? This could be gaining clarity on a specific issue, understanding your emotions better, or exploring your values and goals.

3. Take a few deep breaths to center yourself and bring your focus inward.

4. Start journaling with the following prompts:

• Reflect on a recent situation or event that triggered strong emotions in you. Describe the event in detail, including the people involved, the setting, and the emotions you experienced.

• Explore the underlying reasons for your emotional reaction. Ask yourself why this event affected you so deeply. What values or beliefs were challenged or affirmed? What past experiences might have contributed to your response?

• Consider alternative perspectives. Imagine how someone else involved in the situation might have experienced it differently. How might their thoughts, feelings, or intentions differ from your own?

• Explore any patterns or recurring themes in your emotional reactions. Are there certain situations or triggers that consistently evoke strong emotions? What do these patterns reveal about your values, fears, or desires?

• Identify any lessons or insights you gained from this self-reflection. How can you apply these insights to future situations? What actions or changes might you consider to align your behavior with your values?

5. Allow yourself to write freely and openly without judgment. Let your thoughts and emotions flow onto the paper.

6. After journaling, take a moment to reread what you wrote. Notice any patterns, common themes, or key realizations that emerge.

7. Consider how you can integrate these insights into your life. Are there specific actions you can take or changes you can make to align your behavior with your values and promote personal growth?

Remember, self-reflection is an ongoing practice, so feel free to revisit this exercise regularly to deepen your understanding of yourself and continue your personal growth journey.

Reducing Stress and Enhancing Emotional Well-being:

MINDFULNESS AND MEDITATION have been shown to reduce stress and enhance emotional well-being. When combined with journaling, these practices offer a powerful means of managing and releasing stress, cultivating emotional resilience, and fostering a greater sense of calm and balance. Men can use their journaling practice to explore stress triggers, identify sources of emotional tension, and develop strategies for self-care and stress reduction.

Here's a practical exercise to reduce stress and enhance emotional well-being:

1. Find a quiet and comfortable space where you can relax and focus on yourself.
2. Begin by practicing deep breathing. Take slow, deep breaths in through your nose, allowing your abdomen to expand, and exhale slowly through your mouth. Repeat this deep breathing pattern for a few minutes, focusing on the sensation of each breath.
3. Take out your journal or a piece of paper and start a gratitude list. Write down at least five things you are grateful for in your life. These can be simple things like a sunny day, a good cup of coffee, a gift of life, or supportive friends and family. Reflect on the positive aspects of your life and the things that bring you joy.
4. Now, shift your focus to your emotions. Write a letter to yourself, expressing any stress, worries, or negative emotions you are currently experiencing. Be honest and open about how you feel, allowing yourself to release any pent-up emotions onto the paper. You can also write about any challenges you are facing or things that are causing you stress.

5. Once you've finished writing the letter, read it aloud to yourself. Take a moment to acknowledge and validate your emotions without judgment. Remind yourself that it's okay to feel these emotions and that you're taking a positive step towards managing them.

6. Now, flip to a new page in your journal and write a response to your letter from a compassionate and supportive perspective. Imagine you are a close friend or a compassionate mentor offering advice and encouragement. Write down positive affirmations, self-compassionate statements, and words of wisdom to uplift yourself.

7. Reflect on the emotions you expressed in your initial letter and identify one or two actionable steps you can take to address them or alleviate the associated stress. These could be self-care activities, reaching out for support, or making changes in your routine or environment. Write down these action steps.

8. Finally, end the exercise by revisiting your gratitude list. Reflect on the things you wrote down and allow yourself to feel a sense of gratitude and appreciation for them. Take a moment to savor these positive emotions.

9. Keep your journal and revisit it whenever you need to release emotions, gain perspective, or remind yourself of the things you're grateful for.

By regularly engaging in this journaling exercise, you can effectively reduce stress, enhance emotional well-being, and develop a greater sense of self-awareness and self-compassion. Remember, journaling is a personal practice, and there are no right or wrong answers. Allow yourself to be open, honest, and gentle with yourself throughout the process.

Enhancing Creativity and Intuition:

THE INTEGRATION OF mindfulness, meditation, and journaling can unlock the realms of creativity and intuition. By quieting the mind, men can tap into their deeper wisdom, allowing fresh perspectives and innovative ideas to emerge during the journaling process. Mindful journaling enables the exploration of creative solutions, the discovery of hidden insights, and the nurturing of intuition, leading to a more enriching and transformative journaling experience.

Here's a practical exercise for enhancing creativity and intuition:

1. Find a quiet and comfortable space where you can relax and focus without distractions.
2. Take a few deep breaths and center yourself in the present moment.
3. Choose a creative medium that resonates with you, such as painting, writing, music, or even cooking.
4. Without overthinking or judging, allow yourself to freely express your thoughts and emotions through the chosen medium. Let go of any expectations and embrace the process of exploration.
5. Engage in a creative exercise that encourages intuitive expression. Here are a few examples:

• Free Writing: Set a timer for 10-15 minutes and write continuously without stopping or censoring yourself. Let your thoughts flow freely, trusting your intuition to guide your writing.

• Collage Making: Gather magazines, newspapers, or any materials you find inspiring. Cut out images, words, and phrases that resonate with you, and intuitively arrange them on a board or paper to create a collage that represents your current state of mind.

• Improvisation: If you play a musical instrument, spend some time improvising melodies or experimenting with different chords and rhythms. Allow yourself to follow your intuition and let the music flow naturally.

• Creative Movement: Put on some music and let your body move freely and spontaneously. Allow your intuition to guide your movements, exploring different rhythms, gestures, and expressions.

6. After engaging in the creative exercise, take a moment to reflect and journal about your experience. Consider the following prompts:

• How did it feel to engage in the creative process without constraints or judgment?

• Did you notice any intuitive insights or ideas emerging during the exercise?

• What surprised you about your creative expression?

• How can you incorporate more intuitive and creative practices into your daily life?

1. Repeat this exercise regularly, exploring different creative mediums and exercises. Allow yourself to embrace the joy of creative expression and trust in your intuition to guide you.

By engaging in this activity, you can tap into your ingrained creativity and intuition, opening up new prospects for self-articulation and problem-solving.Over time, this practice can enhance your overall creative capacities and consolidate your connection to your intuitive wisdom.

Chapter 8 Group Journaling for Men's Mental Health

Group journaling is a profitable system for enhancing men's internal well- being and self-development, complementing individual journaling. This chapter explores the advantages of group journaling and offers advice on discovering or establishing a journaling group, organizing group journaling sessions, and cultivating a supportive and satisfying ambience for cooperative journaling interactions.

1. Discovering or Creating a Journaling Group:

FINDING OR CREATING a journaling group specifically acclimatized for men can give a sense of fellowship and shared experiences. Men can explore regional community centers, libraries, or online platforms to connect with suchlike-inclined individuals interested in journaling. Alternatively, they can initiate their own journaling group by reaching out to friends, associates, or acquaintances who may be interested in joining. Group members should share a common interest in individual growth, mental well-being, and a goodwill to engage in open and supportive conversations.

2. Structuring Group Journaling Sessions:

GROUP JOURNALING SESSIONS can be structured in various customs to maximize the benefits and nurture a sense of connection.Some ideas for structuring sessions include:

• Opening Reflection: Begin each session with a brief reflection or awareness exercise to create a shared space of presence and focus.

• Individual Journaling Time: Allocate a specific amount of time for each party to engage in individual journaling, allowing for individual reflection and expression.

• Group Participating: After the individual journaling period, encourage participants to partake their thoughts, perceptivity, or any challenges they encountered during the process. This sharing can be voluntary, ensuring a safe and non-judgmental space for each participant.

• Guided Conversations: Incorporate guided conversations grounded on specific journaling prompts or themes to nurture deeper exploration and meaningful conversations within the group.

• Peer Support and Feedback: Encourage participants to give supportive feedback and confirmation to each other's journaling experiences, emphasizing the significance of active listening and empathy.

3. Benefits of Group Journaling:

GROUP JOURNALING OFFERS several unique benefits for men's mental health:

• Shared Connection and Support: Group journaling creates a sense of community, allowing men to connect with others who may share similar struggles or experiences. This participated connection provides a support system where individuals can offer boost, understanding, and confirmation.

● Diverse Perspectives: Group journaling exposes participants to different perspectives, allowing for a broader range of perceptivity and learning opportunities. Different backgrounds, life experiences, and viewpoints can improve the journaling process and elevate individual growth.

● Responsibility and Motivation: The group setting provides a sense of responsibility and motivation, as participants can share their ambitions, progress, and challenges. This shared commitment encourages individuals to stay motivated, overcome obstacles, and celebrate accomplishments.

● Enhanced Self-Reflection: Group journaling can consolidate self-reflection by supplying an external perspective on one's thoughts and experiences. Through shared conversations, participants gain perceptivity into their own feelings, beliefs, and actions, guiding to expanded self-mindfulness and particular development.

● Skill Building: Group journaling offers opportunities for developing active listening, empathy, and effective communication skills. Engaging in thoughtful conversations and providing constructive feedback enhances interpersonal skills and promotes healthy relations within the group and beyond.

4. Fostering a Supportive Environment:

TO CREATE A SUCCESSFUL and supportive group journaling experience, regard the following:

● Establish Trust: Create an atmosphere of trust and confidentiality, highlighting the significance of esteeming each other's privacy and maintaining a safe space for sharing individual thoughts and experiences.

● Encourage Active Participation: Foster an inclusive environment where all participants feel comfortable sharing their thoughts and engaging indiscussions.bEncourage functional participation while esteeming individuals' comfort situations.

● Exercise Empathy: Cultivate a culture of empathy and understanding within the group. Encourage participants to laboriously hear, authenticate each other's experiences.

Chapter 9 Success Stories: Real Men Who Have Benefited from Journaling

IN THIS CHAPTER, WE will explore true- life case studies of men who have integrated journaling into their mental health routine and witnessed significant benefits. These stories deliver inspiration and practical perceptivity into how journaling can be used as a tool for emotional regulation and self-discovery.

Case Study 1: John

John is a 35- time-old man who has suffered from anxiety and depression for numerous years.He struggled to open up to friends and family, and he constantly felt as if he was bearing his feelings alone.He decided to attempt journaling after hearing about its advantages.

John began by outlining his concerns and anxieties, and then confronting them with facts to the contrary.He also utilized reflective writing to investigate the root reasons of his anxiety and depression, such as work-related stress and childhood trauma.Over time, he improved his self-awareness and emotional regulation, and he felt more empowered to take charge of his mental health.

Case Study 2: Mike

Mike is a 45-year-old gentleman who experienced a terrible circumstance in his early twenties. He suffered with memories and hypervigilance at times and found it difficult to trust others. He decided to explore journaling as a means to continue his recovery journey after attending therapy.

Mike utilized his journal as a secure space to express his feelings and process difficult memories. He also used gratitude journaling to concentrate on the positive aspects of his life and cultivate a sense of hope for the future. Through journaling, Mike was able to develop a prime sense of self-compassion and forgiveness, and felt more connected to others.

Case Study 3: Mark

Mark is a 28-year-old nobleman who has spent his whole life dealing with self-doubt and negative self-talk. He failed to honor his own strengths and successes, and he was constantly concerned about missing out on opportunities. He decided to try journaling after reading about the advantages.

Mark used his notebook to fight negative ideas and replace them with positive affirmations.He also utilized free jotting to examine his own beliefs and ambitions, as well as to establish a strong sense of purpose and meaning.Over time, he acquired a more positive self-image and gained confidence in his talents. He is more assured of his ability.

Case Study 4: Tom

Tom, a 50-year-old man, suffered from work-related stress and burnout. He struggled to open from work and constantly felt overwhelmed by his obligations.He chose to attempt journaling as a stress-management approach after attending a mental health program.

Tom employed his journal to reflect on his priorities and find places where he might delegate or request assistance.He also used suggestions and activities to enrich his work-life balance and self-care.Tom was capable to have better control over his workload and feel more invigorated and driven through journaling.

Case Study 5: Sipho

Sipho is a 30-year-old guy who has suffered from addiction and substance abuse. He struggled to stop the cycle of addiction and frequently felt embarrassed and alienated. He decided to attempt writing as a means to keep focused on his goals after attending a rehabilitation program.

Sipho employed his journal as a route to track his progress and celebrate his successes.He also used reflective journaling to explore the underpinning causes of his addiction and develop managing strategies for handling triggers. Through journaling, Sipho was able to develop a prime sense of self-mindfulness and responsibility, and feel more empowered to stay sober.

Conclusion

Summing up the benefits of journaling for men's mental health and instill discipline

In conclusion, journaling may be an effective way for men in perfecting their mental health and managing their emotions. Men may gain the advantages of this simple yet powerful exercise by learning the exploration behind jotting, overcoming common hurdles, exploring new ways, and exercising journaling to tackle specific mental health concerns. Journaling is a feasible alternative for anybody trying to improve their overall well-being, as substantiated by the success stories of real men who have included it into their mental health situations.

Encouragement to give journaling a try

JOURNALING MAY BE A terrific approach to educate discipline and assist you prioritize your mental health. The benefits of journaling are egregious and numerous, and there's no better time to start than now. Whether you choose gratitude journaling, reflective journaling, free jotting, or any other type of journaling, the pivotal thing is to begin nearly and to be consistent. So go ahead and pick up a pen and paper, or buy our generated journal designed simply for guys, along with various interactive exercises, and see where the power of jotting may lead you .